HBJ TREASURY OF LITERATURE

THE DEEP BLUE SEA

SENIOR AUTHORS
ROGER C. FARR
DOROTHY S. STRICKLAND

AUTHORS
RICHARD F. ABRAHAMSON
ELLEN BOOTH CHURCH
BARBARA BOWEN COULTER
MARGARET A. GALLEGO
JUDITH L. IRVIN
KAREN KUTIPER
JUNKO YOKOTA LEWIS
DONNA M. OGLE
TIMOTHY SHANAHAN
PATRICIA SMITH

SENIOR CONSULTANTS
BERNICE E. CULLINAN
W. DORSEY HAMMOND
ASA G. HILLIARD III

CONSULTANTS
ALONZO A. CRIM
ROLANDO R. HINOJOSA-SMITH
LEE BENNETT HOPKINS
ROBERT J. STERNBERG

HARCOURT BRACE & COMPANY
Orlando Atlanta Austin Boston San Francisco Chicago Dallas New York
Toronto London

Printed in the United States of America

ISBN 0-15-301361-3

3 4 5 6 7 8 9 10   048   96   95   94   93

Acknowledgments

For permission to reprint copyrighted material, grateful acknowledgment is made to the following sources:

Jose Aruego and Ariane Dewey: Illustrations by Jose Aruego and Ariane Dewey from *Sea Frog, City Frog* by Dorothy O. Van Woerkom. Illustrations copyright © 1985 by Jose Aruego and Ariane Dewey.

Childrens Press, Inc.: Cover illustration by Anne Sikorski from *Country Mouse and City Mouse* by Pat McKissack. Copyright © 1985 by Childrens Press®, Inc. Cover illustration by Lois Axeman from *A Tasting Party* by Jane Belk Moncure. Copyright © 1982 by Childrens Press®, Inc.

Dial Books for Young Readers, a division of Penguin Books USA Inc.: Cover illustration by Simms Taback from *Fishy Riddles* by Katy Hall and Lisa Eisenberg. Illustration copyright © 1983 by Simms Taback. "Vegetables" from *Lionel at Large* by Stephen Krensky, illustrated by Susanna Natti. Text copyright © 1986 by Stephen Krensky; illustrations copyright © 1986 by Susanna Natti.

Dutton Children's Books, a division of Penguin Books USA Inc.: *Punky Goes Fishing* by Sally G. Ward. Copyright © 1991 by Sally G. Ward.

Greenwillow Books, a division of William Morrow & Company, Inc.: The Doorbell Rang by Pat Hutchins. Copyright © 1986 by Pat Hutchins.

Harcourt Brace Jovanovich, Inc.: Cover illustration from *Fish Eyes: A Book You Can Count On* by Lois Ehlert. Copyright © 1990 by Lois Ehlert.

HarperCollins Publishers: "Cookies" from *Frog and Toad Together* by Arnold Lobel. Copyright © 1972 by Arnold Lobel. Cover illustration from *Mouse Soup* by Arnold Lobel. Copyright © 1977 by Arnold Lobel. "Little Bear and Owl" from *Father Bear Comes Home* by Else Holmelund Minarik, illustrated by Maurice Sendak. Text copyright © 1959 by Else Holmelund Minarik; illustrations copyright © 1959 by Maurice Sendak. "All of Our Noses Are Here" from *All of Our Noses Are Here and Other Noodle Tales* by Alvin Schwartz, illustrated by Karen Ann Weinhaus. Text copyright © 1985 by Alvin Schwartz; illustrations copyright © 1985 by Karen Ann Weinhaus.

Little, Brown and Company: *The Cake That Mack Ate* by Rose Robart, illustrated by Maryann Kovalski. Text copyright © 1986 by Rose Robart; illustrations copyright © 1986 by Maryann Kovalski.

Little, Brown and Company, in association with Joy Street Books: *D.W. All Wet* by Marc Brown. Copyright © 1988 by Marc Brown.

Lothrop, Lee & Shepard Books, a division of William Morrow & Company, Inc.: "Seaside" from *Out and About* by Shirley Hughes. Text copyright © 1988 by Shirley Hughes. Cover illustration by Jan Ormerod from *Eat Up, Gemma* by Sarah Hayes. Illustration copyright © 1988 by Jan Ormerod.

Gina Maccoby Literary Agency: From *Nuts To You & Nuts To Me* (Retitled: "Cookie Cutters") by Mary Ann Hoberman. Text copyright © 1974 by Mary Ann Hoberman. Published by Alfred A. Knopf.

Macmillan Publishing Company: Cover illustration from *Hugo at the Park* by Anne Rockwell. Copyright © 1990 by Anne Rockwell. *Sea Frog, City Frog* by Dorothy O. Van Woerkom. Text copyright © 1975 by Dorothy O. Van Woerkom.

N. Van Wright Mellage: "To Catch a Fish" by N. Van Wright Mellage. Text © 1990 by Nanette Van Wright Mellage.

Morrow Junior Books, a division of William Morrow & Company, Inc.: Cover illustration from *Yellow Ball* by Molly Bang. Copyright © 1991 by Molly Bang.

Orchard Books, New York: Cover illustration by Ruth Tietjen Councell from *Country Bear's Good Neighbor* by Larry Dane Brimner. Illustration copyright © 1988 by Ruth Tietjen Councell.

G. P. Putnam's Sons: Cover illustration from *Old Mother Hubbard* by Colin and Jacqui Hawkins. Copyright © 1984 by Colin and Jacqui Hawkins.

Raintree Publishers, a division of Steck-Vaughn Company: From *Peanut Butter, Apple Butter, Cinnamon Toast* (Retitled: "Food Riddles for You") by Argentina Palacios, illustrated by Ben Mahan. © 1990 by American Teacher Publications. Published by Steck-Vaughn Company.

Random House, Inc.: "The Fish That Goes Fishing" from *Fish Do the Strangest Things* by Leonora and Arthur Hornblow. Text copyright © 1966 by Random House, Inc.

Elizabeth Roach: "Cookies" from *Rhymes About Us* by Marchette Chute. Text copyright 1974 by Marchette Chute.

Jean Stangl: "Peanut Butter Balls" (Retitled: "Make Peanut Butter Balls") from *The No-Cook Cookery Cookbook* by Jean Stangl. Text copyright © 1976 by Mary Jean Stangl.

Sterling Publishing Co., Inc., 387 Park Ave. S., New York, NY 10016: "A Sailor Went to Sea, Sea, Sea" from *Musical Games for Children of All Ages* by Esther L. Nelson. Text © 1976 by Esther L. Nelson.

Viking Penguin, a division of Penguin Books USA Inc.: From *In My Mother's House* by Ann Nolan Clark, illustrated by Velino Herrera. Copyright 1941 by Ann Nolan Clark, renewed © 1969 by Ann Nolan Clark.

Franklin Watts, Inc.: "Water Signs" from *North American Indian Sign Language* by Karen Liptak. Text copyright © 1990 by Karen Liptak.

Handwriting models in this program have been used with permission of the publisher, Zaner-Bloser, Inc., Columbus, OH.

Dear Reader,

Reading can take you many places. Come and sail on the deep blue sea. These stories will let you meet new faces. You can learn Indian water signs. You will read a Japanese folktale about two silly frogs. You will meet many different animals and people in this book.

All kinds of people make up a beautiful world. In the same way, all the stories you will read fit together to form a beautiful book. Set sail and get ready!

Sincerely,
The Authors

C O N T E N T S

UNIT ONE / WATER WAYS 8

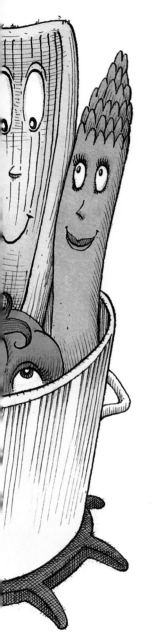

UNIT ONE

WATER·WAYS

"If all the seas were one sea
what a great sea it would be . . ."
Mother Goose

Do you like the water? Many people do. Being around water is lots of fun. What do you like to do near water? Maybe you like to ride in a boat on the water. Did you know that the Haida Indians liked to build beautiful boats? As you read these stories, you'll meet many others who like to do things near water.

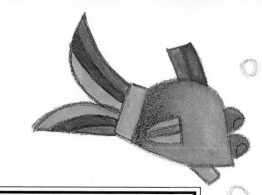

BOOKSHELF

YELLOW BALL
BY MOLLY BANG

A yellow ball is left too close to the water. It floats out to sea. Follow the yellow ball as it travels high and low, above and below, and into a terrible storm.

AWARD-WINNING AUTHOR

HBJ LIBRARY BOOK

COUNTRY MOUSE AND CITY MOUSE
BY PATRICIA & FREDERICK McKISSACK

City Mouse and Country Mouse visit each other's homes. Find out what the mice learn from their trips.

10

FISHY RIDDLES
BY KATY HALL AND LISA EISENBERG

"Why are fish so smart? Because they are always in schools!" Dive into these fishy riddles. You'll have a "whale" of a time! AWARD-WINNING AUTHORS

HUGO AT THE PARK
BY ANNE ROCKWELL

Hugo the dog and his owner go to the park to enjoy a beautiful day. Hugo has a lot of fun singing, running, and playing in the park. Find out what happens when Hugo says hello to a swan. AWARD-WINNING AUTHOR

FISH EYES: A BOOK YOU CAN COUNT ON
WRITTEN AND ILLUSTRATED BY LOIS EHLERT

"Would you wish to be a fish?" Swim through this book, and count the fish along the way. If you look closely, you'll find a friendly fish that will help you along. NEW YORK TIMES BEST ILLUSTRATED

11

SAND AND SEA

Do you like to play in the water? Read a story and a poem about fun in the water. Then have fun with Indian water signs.

"It's too hot!" shouted D.W.

"That's why we came to the beach,"
said Mother.

"I don't like the beach," said D.W.

"And I don't like to get wet."

"Here's a good spot," said Father.

"When are we leaving?" asked D.W.

"We just got here," said Mother.
"Come on, D.W. Take off your robe,"
said Arthur.
"Last one in is a rotten egg!"
"I'm not playing," said D.W.
"I don't want to get sunburned.
And no splashing!"

"Come on in," called Arthur. "The water's great!"

"I don't want to," said D.W. "I don't like the water."

"You haven't even tried it," said Father.

"Is it time to go yet?" asked D.W.

"Not yet," said Arthur.
"I'm going for a walk."
"Me, too!" said D.W.
"You walk. I'll ride.
Help me up!"

"But I can't see!" said Arthur.
"You don't need to," said D.W.
"I'll tell you where to go."

"Go!" she said.

"Where are we going?" asked Arthur.

"It's a surprise," said D.W.
"Keep walking. Now turn left.
Arthur, I said left. Turn left!"
cried D.W.
"Not that way! Stop!"

SPLASH!

"Help! Help!" screamed D.W. "I can't swim!"

"You don't have to," said Arthur.
"Just stand up."

Then D.W. dipped,

floated,

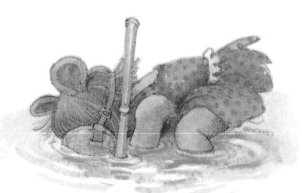

flipped,

flopped,

squirted,

splashed,

and dunked.

"Time to go!" called Father.
"Let's come back tomorrow!" said D.W.

THINK IT OVER

1. What made D.W. change her mind about the beach?

2. How did Arthur get D.W. into the water?

WRITE

Write about what might happen if D.W. comes back to the beach.

WATER SIGNS

from North American Indian Sign Language

BY KAREN LIPTAK

illustrations by
Scott Scheidly • Ann Morton Hubbard

Make the Indian water signs
that you see in the pictures. Try to
speak to a friend using these signs.

WATER (DRINK)

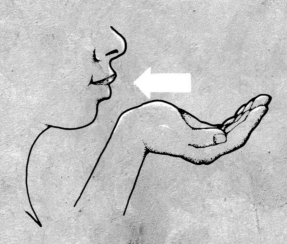

LAKE

RIVER

BOAT

CANOE

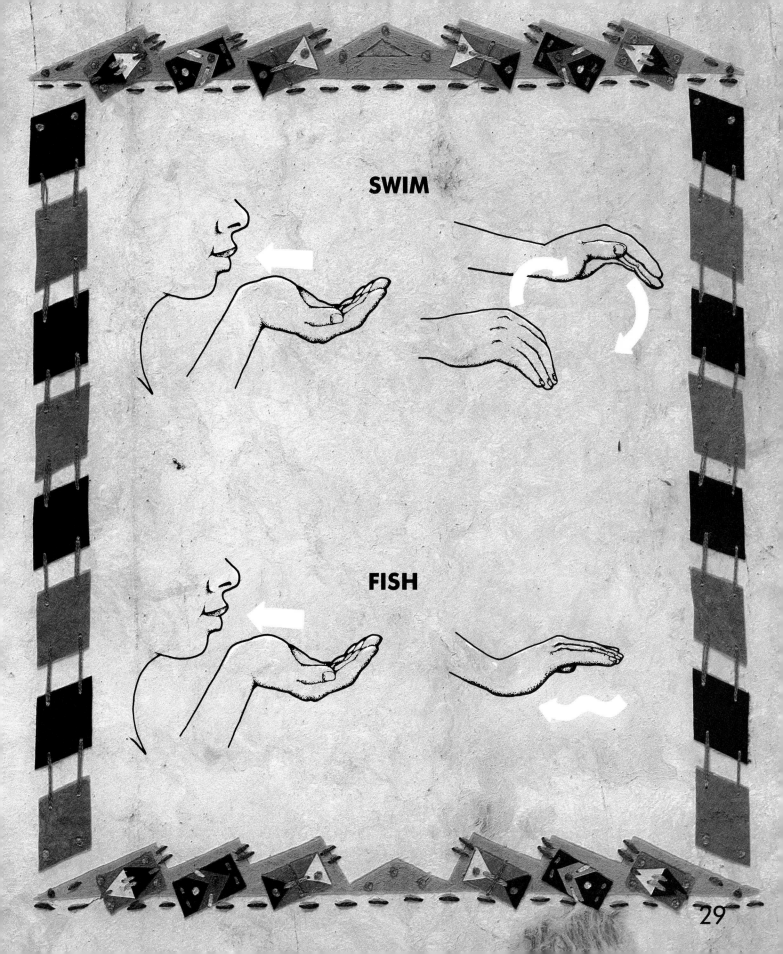

SWIM

FISH

29

SEASIDE

Sand in the sandwiches,
Sand in the tea,
Flat, wet sand running
Down to the sea.
Pools full of seaweed,
Shells and stones,
Damp bathing suits
And ice-cream cones.

Waves pouring in
To a sand-castle moat.
Mend the defenses!
Now we're afloat!
Water's for splashing,
Sand is for play,
A day by the sea
Is the best kind of day.

Shirley Hughes

Edward Henry Potthast
1857–1927
Children on the Beach
Hirschorne Collection

SAND AND SEA

What words would you use to tell about a day at the beach?

· ·

If you could spend a day at the beach, what would you do?

· ·

WRITER'S WORKSHOP Write a story about what you might do or see in the water. Tell what you would do first, next, and last. Use some of the words from "Water Signs."

SOMETHING SILLY

Think about some silly things.
Have you read any funny stories?
Here are some stories that can
make you laugh.

CONTENTS

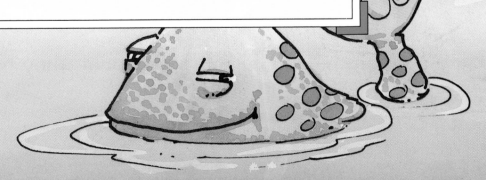

33

All of Our Noses Are Here

from ALL OF OUR NOSES ARE HERE AND OTHER NOODLE TALES

retold by Alvin Schwartz

pictures by Karen Ann Weinhaus

The Browns went for a ride in their rowboat.
When the sun began to go down, they rowed
back to shore.

34

"Everyone line up," said Mr. Brown.
"Let us see if anybody fell out of
the boat.
One is here.
Two are here.
Three are here.
And four are here."

"But we are five," said Mrs. Brown.
"I think I counted wrong,"
said Mr. Brown. "I will count again.

One is here.

Two are here.

Three are here.

And four are here."

"Only four?" asked Mrs. Brown.

"Yes," said Mr. Brown.

"One of us is missing."

Mrs. Brown began to cry.

So did the others.

"Why are all of you crying?"
a fisherman asked.

"Five of us went rowing," said Mr. Brown.

"But only four came back."

"Are you sure?" the fisherman asked.

Mr. Brown counted again.

Again he counted only four.

"I know what is wrong,"
said the fisherman.

"You forgot to count yourself."

"I will try again," said Mr. Brown.

"One is here.

Two are here.

Three are here.

And four are here.

And five are here.

And SIX are here!"

"But there should be five,"
said Mrs. Brown.

"No," said Mr. Brown.

"Now we are six."

"But I do not see anybody else,"
said Mrs. Brown.

They looked in the rowboat

and under the dock

and up in the trees

and behind all the bushes,

but they did not find anyone.

"Come out! Come out!

Whoever you are!"

Mr. Brown shouted.

The others joined in,

but nobody came out.

When the fisherman

heard the shouting,

he went to see what

was wrong.

"Now there are six of us

instead of five," said Mr. Brown.

"But we cannot find

this extra person."

"Are you sure there are six?"
the fisherman asked.
Mr. Brown counted again,
and again he counted six.
"You are doing it all wrong,"
said the fisherman.
"You counted yourself twice.
Let me show you
the right way to count.

Everybody, get down on your
hands and knees.
Now stick your noses
into the mud
and pull them out.

Now count the holes your
noses made."
Mr. Brown counted.
"One is here.
Two are here.
Three are here.
Four are here.
And *five* are here.
All of our noses are here!" he said.
"Now we can go home."

44

THINK IT OVER

1. What made this a funny story?

2. Why is the title a good one for this story?

WRITE

Write about another silly thing the Browns might do on an outing.

Sea Frog, City Frog

A JAPANESE FOLKTALE

BY DOROTHY O. VAN WOERKOM

ILLUSTRATED BY JOSE ARUEGO AND ARIANE DEWEY

Sea Frog lived in a bog by the sea.
City Frog lived in a pond in the city.
One day when the sun was bright,
Sea Frog said, "How nice it would be
to see the city!"
And City Frog said, "I would
like to see the sea!"

47

So City Frog jumped
out of his pond.
He hopped
down the road
to the sea.

And Sea Frog jumped
out of his bog.
He hopped up the road
to the city.

The two frogs
hopped for a day
and a night.
At last they came
to a hill.

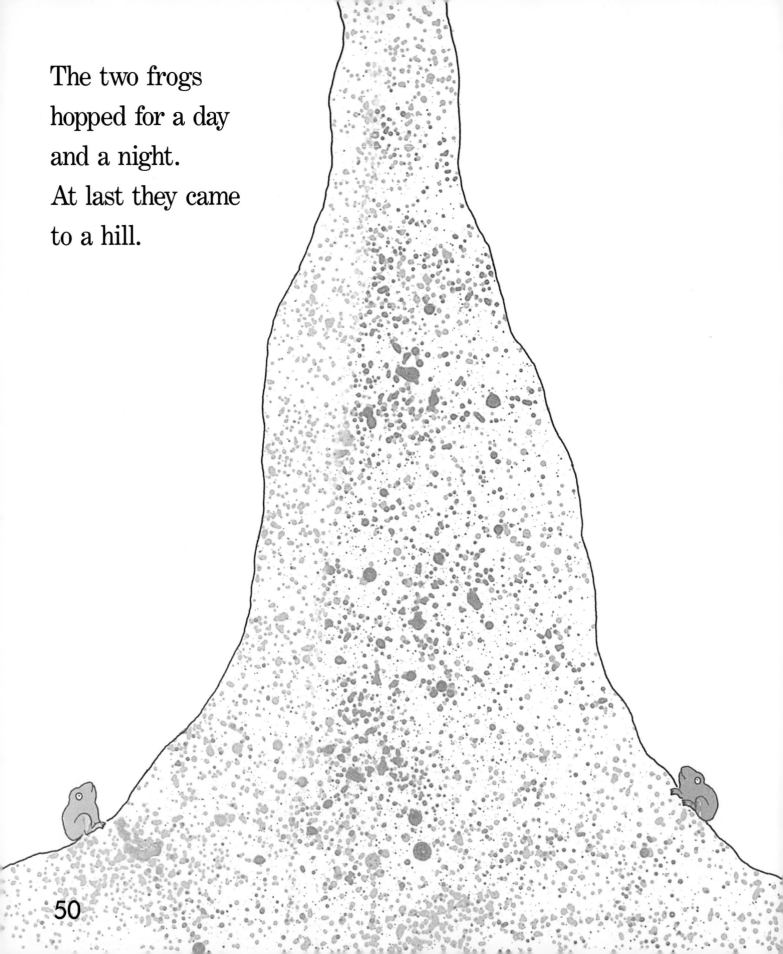

Up one side
of the hill
hopped City Frog.
How tired he was!

Up the other side
of the hill
hopped Sea Frog.
And he was tired!

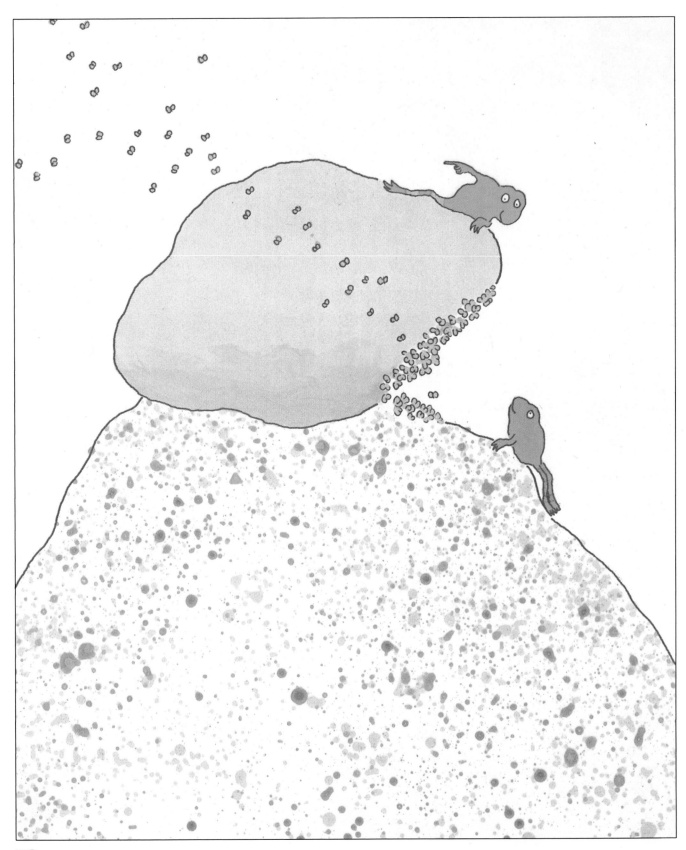

The two frogs met
at the top of the hill.
"Hello!" said City Frog.
"I am from the city.
I am going to the sea.
Where are you from?
Where are you going?"
Sea Frog said,
"I am from the sea,
and I am going to the city."
"How nice that we should meet,"
said City Frog.
"Let us rest and talk for an hour."

So they sat
in the shade
of a big rock.
They talked.
They caught bugs
on their long tongues.

They even took a nap.
Then City Frog woke up.
"I wish," he said,
"that we were tall."
Sea Frog opened one eye.
"What good would that do?"
he said.

"Would it get you
to the sea, and me
to the city?"
"No," said City Frog.
"But here we are
on top of this hill.
Now, if we were tall,
we could see far away."
"How smart you are!"
Sea Frog said.
"And we can do it!
We can make ourselves tall."

55

"Show me how we can do that,"
said City Frog.
"Like this," said Sea Frog.
Sea Frog stood up with his
front legs in the air.
"We can make ourselves tall
if we hold onto each other!"
So the frogs stood up on their
long hind legs.
With their short front legs
they held onto each other.

"I can see a long way!"
said City Frog.
"So can I," Sea Frog said.

So City Frog turned his nose
to the sea.
And Sea Frog turned his nose
to the city.
The poor, silly frogs!
Their noses were turned
where they wanted to go.
But their great eyes—which were
at the back of their heads—
only saw where they had been!

"Oh, my!" said Sea Frog.
"The city is just like the sea!"

"Dear me!" said City Frog.
"The sea is just like the city!"

So the frogs went home again. And they never knew
that the sea is not at all like the city, and the city
is not at all like the sea.

THINK IT OVER

1. Where were the frogs going when they met?

2. What did the frogs really see?

WRITE

Draw a picture to show what City Frog thought the sea
looked like. Write about your picture.

Jose Aruego and Ariane Dewey

Jose Aruego and Ariane Dewey made the pictures for <u>Sea Frog, City Frog.</u>

Jose Aruego grew up in the Philippines. His family had birds, dogs, cats, chickens, roosters, pigs, ducks, and horses. This may be why Mr. Aruego loves to draw animals. He says his animals' funny faces often make him laugh while he works.

Ariane Dewey was born in Chicago, Illinois. When she was in the fourth grade, she wrote a book and drew the pictures. It was then that she knew she wanted to become a painter. Ms. Dewey loves color. She adds the colors to Jose Aruego's pictures.

Because Ariane Dewey likes to paint and Jose Aruego likes to draw, they work very well together.

A Sailor Went to Sea, Sea, Sea

by Esther L. Nelson

A sailor went to sea, sea, sea,
To see what he could see, see, see, but
All that he could see, see, see,
Was the bottom of the deep blue
sea, sea, sea.

SOMETHING SILLY

What would the fisherman tell the frogs if he met them on top of the hill? What would the frogs do?

· ·

Who do you think are sillier, the Browns or the frogs? Why do you think so?

· ·

WRITER'S WORKSHOP   Pretend you are Sea Frog or City Frog. Write a letter to the other frog. Tell about where you live and what you see, hear, and smell there.

63

GOING FISHING

Would you like to go fishing? Read
about fishing and about some fish
that were caught!

Punky Goes Fishing

by SALLY G. WARD

Punky was sleeping over at her grandparents' house.

"Grampy," she asked, "may I go fishing with you tomorrow?"

"Well, Punky," said Grampy, "let me think about it. Fishing is serious business, you know."

The next morning, Punky had just finished
her breakfast when Grampy surprised her.
"What do you say, Punky . . . want to try
some fishing?"
So they prepared their lunches, and Punky
put on her old clothes.
"I'm bringing a towel, in case you get
wet," said Grampy.

Grampy gave Punky a little fishing pole.
"It's just the right size for you, Punky,"
he said. "And here's
my great big one for
catching the big fish."

"I want you to wear this life jacket, dear,
so Grampy knows you're safe."
"Don't you need to
wear one, Grampy?"
asked Punky.
"Oh no,"
Grampy laughed.
"I never fall in."

Out on the water, Punky watched the houses
get smaller.

"It's so quiet out here, Grampy," she said.

"That's why I like it," Grampy replied.

"And here's where we stop, Punky.

The water is only up to my middle.

Plenty safe. I'll set the anchor."

The anchor went in easily.
But so did Grampy's lunch.

"That's all right, Grampy. You can
share mine."
"Thank you, Punky," said Grampy.

Grampy got the poles ready,
and they sat back to wait.
"Any nibbles yet, Grampy?"

"Nope . . . well,
wait a minute. . . ."
"Wow, Grampy.
You caught a teeny one."
"Yup," he said, "that one
goes right back in."

The fish went in easily.
But so did one of the oars.

72

"Good thing I brought my waders," said
Grampy. "When we're done, I'll *pull* us
back to shore."
"I'm hungry, Grampy. Let's have lunch."
"Good idea, Punky. I'm hungry, too."

After lunch Grampy said, "Let's try one
more time, all right?"
"Sure," said Punky. "Only, can I fix
my own hook? I want to try a little piece
of the leftover fig bar on it."

"Ha ha," laughed Grampy. "Never heard of a fish who wanted to take a bite of a fig bar. Take it from me. Your old grandpa knows what's what. Especially when it comes to fishing."

"Grampy! I think I've got something!
GRAMPY! I _know_ I've got something!"
"Keep reeling, Punky. I'm coming."
"Looks like a whopper! GOTCHA!"

The fish stayed in the net.
But Grampy went over.

"Wow, Grampy!
Wait till Grammy sees
what I caught."

It was time to go home.

"Grampy! You got a fish, too!
Can we go again tomorrow?"

THINK IT OVER

1. Who was a better fisher, Grampy or Punky? Why do you think so?

2. How do you know Punky had fun fishing with Grampy?

WRITE

Pretend you are Punky. Write a letter to your family. Tell them about your fishing trip.

THE FISH THAT GOES FISHING

FROM FISH DO THE STRANGEST THINGS
by Leonora and Arthur Hornblow

People catch many strange fish.
But one of the strangest fish of all
does her own fishing.
She lives down deep in the dark sea.
She is called the deep-sea angler.
The deep-sea angler has
her own fishing rod.
It grows out of the top of
her head and hangs in
front of her mouth.
The tip of her rod shines in
the deep dark water.

This tip is the bait on her fishing rod. Hungry fish see her bait. They think it is something to eat. A hungry fish will swim toward the shiny bait.

The angler opens her wide mouth.
The fish swims closer and closer.
He swims right at the bait. Then the
angler closes her mouth. Snap!
That's the end of that fish.

illustrated by Bernie Knox

82

TO CATCH A FISH

Dana went to catch a fish
He took his fishing pole
And cast his line into the lake
A chocolate cookie was his bait
He sat upon a rock to wait
To catch a great big fish

Suddenly he heard Blub Blub
Two fish stuck out their heads
"Offer us our favorite dishes
Worms or flies or smaller fishes
Maybe then you'll get your wish"
And off they swam, Blub Blub!

Nanette Mellage
illustrated by Floyd Cooper

LITTLE BEAR AND OWL

FROM <u>FATHER BEAR COMES HOME</u>
WRITTEN BY ELSE HOLMELUND MINARIK
PICTURES BY MAURICE SENDAK

ALA
NOTABLE
BOOK

"Little Bear," said Mother Bear,

"can you be my fisherman?"

"Yes, I can," said Little Bear.

"Good," said Mother Bear.

"Will you go down to the river?

Will you catch a fish for us?"

"Yes, I will," said Little Bear.

So Little Bear went down to
the river.

And there he saw Owl.

Owl was sitting on a log.

"Hello, Little Bear," said Owl.

"Hello, Owl," said Little Bear.

"Father Bear is not home.

He is fishing on the ocean.

But Mother Bear wants a fish now,

so I have to catch one."

"Good," said Owl.

"Catch one."

Little Bear fished.

"I have one," he said.

"Is it too little?"

"It looks good to me," said Owl.

"Well," said Little Bear,

"Father Bear can catch big fish.

He sails in a big boat, too."

Owl said,

"Someday you will be a big bear.

You will catch big fish.

And you will sail in a boat,

like Father Bear."

"I know what," said Little Bear.

"We can make believe.

The log can be a boat.

I will be Father Bear.

"You can be you, and we are fishing."

"Where are we fishing?" asked Owl.

"On the ocean," said Little Bear.

"All right," said Owl.

"Hurray!" said Little Bear.

"See what I have."

"What is it?" asked Owl.

"An octopus," said Little Bear.

"Oh," said Owl.

"But see what I have."

"What is it?" asked Little Bear.

"A whale," said Owl.

"But a whale is too big,"
said Little Bear.

"This is a little whale," said Owl.

Just then Mother Bear came along.

"Where is the fish?" she asked.

Little Bear laughed. He said,

"How about an octopus?"

"An octopus!" said Mother Bear.

"Well, then," said Owl,

"how about a little whale?"

"A WHALE!!" said Mother Bear.

"No, thank you. No whale."

"Then how about this fish?"
said Little Bear.

"Yes, thank you," said Mother Bear,
"that is just what I want."
Little Bear said, "You will see.
When I am as big as Father Bear,
I will catch a real octopus."
"Yes, and sail in a real boat,"
said Owl.
"I know it," said Mother Bear.
Owl said, "Little Bear fishes very well."

"Oh, yes," said Mother Bear,
"he fishes very well,
indeed.
"He is a real fisherman,
just like his father."

THINK IT OVER

1. Why did Little Bear make believe he was fishing on a big boat?

2. If you were Little Bear, which fish would you pretend to catch? Why?

WRITE

Write a new title for this story. Draw a picture to go with your title.

GOING FISHING

If you went fishing with Punky and Grampy, what would you tell them?

· ·

Would you like to catch Punky's fish or Little Bear's fish? Why?

· ·

WRITER'S WORKSHOP   Write your own fishing story about Punky, Little Bear, or the deep-sea angler. Tell what happens first, next, and last.

93

CONNECTIONS

BEAUTIFUL BOATS

Long ago, the Haida Indians made big, beautiful boats. Building them was hard work. The Haida carved pictures on their boats. They painted beautiful paintings on their boats, too. Even the oars were carved and painted.

■ Draw a boat like the one in the picture. Draw or paint beautiful pictures on your boat.

ALL KINDS OF BOATS

Boats are used in many different ways. Find pictures of two kinds of boats. How are the boats like those made by the Haida? How are they different? Make a report to show what you have learned.

The Haida built boats like this one.

WHAT FLOATS YOUR BOAT?

Why do you think boats float instead of sinking? What are some other things that float? What are some things that sink? Put some things in water and see what happens. Write what you learn on a chart like this one.

The wind moves a sailboat.

This boat carries many things.

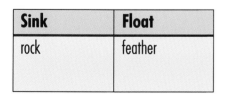

Sink	Float
rock	feather

95

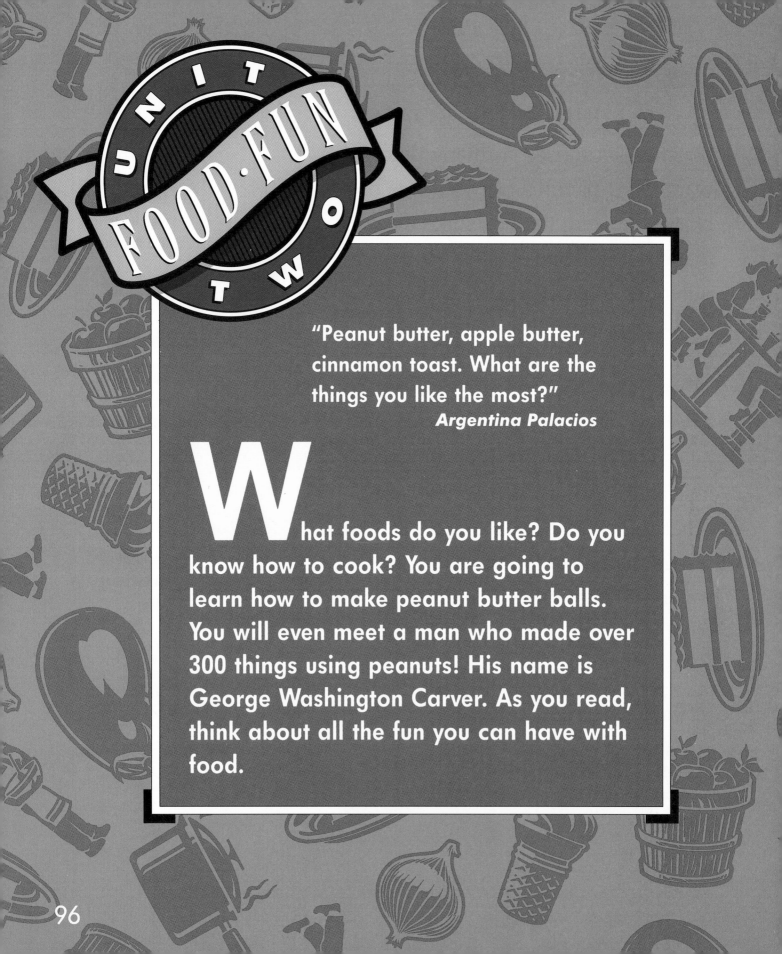

FOOD·FUN

"Peanut butter, apple butter, cinnamon toast. What are the things you like the most?"
Argentina Palacios

What foods do you like? Do you know how to cook? You are going to learn how to make peanut butter balls. You will even meet a man who made over 300 things using peanuts! His name is George Washington Carver. As you read, think about all the fun you can have with food.

EAT UP, GEMMA
BY SARAH HAYES

Everyone says "Eat up, Gemma." But Gemma is a baby who does not want to eat. Gemma's brother thinks of a good idea to get Gemma to "eat up." What's the good idea? Read the book to find out.

HBJ LIBRARY BOOK

MOUSE SOUP
BY ARNOLD LOBEL

"Ah!" said the weasel. "I am going to make mouse soup." "Oh!" said the mouse. "I am going to be mouse soup." Will the poor little mouse become mouse soup? Will he find a way to save himself? CHILDREN'S CHOICE

A TASTING PARTY
BY JANE BELK MONCURE

Have you ever been to a food-tasting party? Wake up your taste buds, and come along. The children in this story taste many kinds of good foods.

COUNTRY BEAR'S GOOD NEIGHBOR
BY LARRY DANE BRIMNER

Country Bear wants to borrow some apples. "Certainly! That's what good neighbors are for," says his neighbor. But Country Bear borrows much more than apples. What is he making with all those things?

OLD MOTHER HUBBARD
BY COLIN AND JACQUI HAWKINS

In this book you can really open the door to Old Mother Hubbard's cupboard. Behind each door you will find Mother Hubbard's dog doing something silly.

99

WHAT'S COOKING?

Do you help cook meals? You can read about how a cake is made. Then you can make your own treat.

C O N T E N T S

The Cake That Mack Ate

Rose Robart · Maryann Kovalski

This is the cake that Mack ate.

This is the egg
That went into the cake
that Mack ate.

This is the hen
That laid the egg,
That went into the cake
that Mack ate.

This is the corn
That fed the hen,
That laid the egg,
That went into the cake
  that Mack ate.

This is the seed
That grew into corn,
That fed the hen,
That laid the egg,
That went into the cake
   that Mack ate.

This is the farmer
Who planted the seed,
That grew into corn,
That fed the hen,
That laid the egg,
That went into the cake
    that Mack ate.

This is the woman
Who married the farmer,
Who planted the seed,
That grew into corn,
That fed the hen,
That laid the egg,
That went into the cake
    that Mack ate.

These are the candles
That lit up the cake,
That was made by the woman,
Who married the farmer,
Who planted the seed,
That grew into corn,
That fed the hen,
That laid the egg,
That went into the cake
    that Mack ate.

This is Mack...

He ate the cake.

THINK IT OVER

1. What kind of cake did Mack eat? How do you know?

2. Why do you think Mack ate the cake?

WRITE

What do you think happened to Mack? Write some sentences that tell.

MAKE PEANUT BUTTER BALLS
BY JEAN STANGL

Mack ate the cake. Now you can make and eat a tasty treat, too!

powdered sugar

powdered milk

peanut butter

❶ Put 2 tablespoons of powdered sugar in a bowl.

❷ Add 2 tablespoons of powdered milk.

❸ Add 4 tablespoons of peanut butter and stir.

graham crackers

❹ Crush 3 graham crackers in a bag.

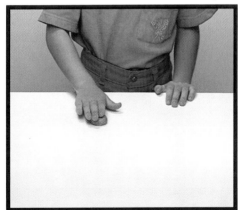

❺ Roll the dough into balls.

❻ Roll the balls in the graham cracker crumbs.

Enjoy your peanut butter balls.

WHAT'S COOKING?

Which would you like to taste—Mack's cake or the peanut butter balls? Tell why.

· ·

Which of the things you read about would you most like to cook? Why?

· ·

WRITER'S WORKSHOP   Write a poem about things you want to cook. You can use the sentence "I want to cook _____ because ___" to help you. Share your poem with classmates.

117

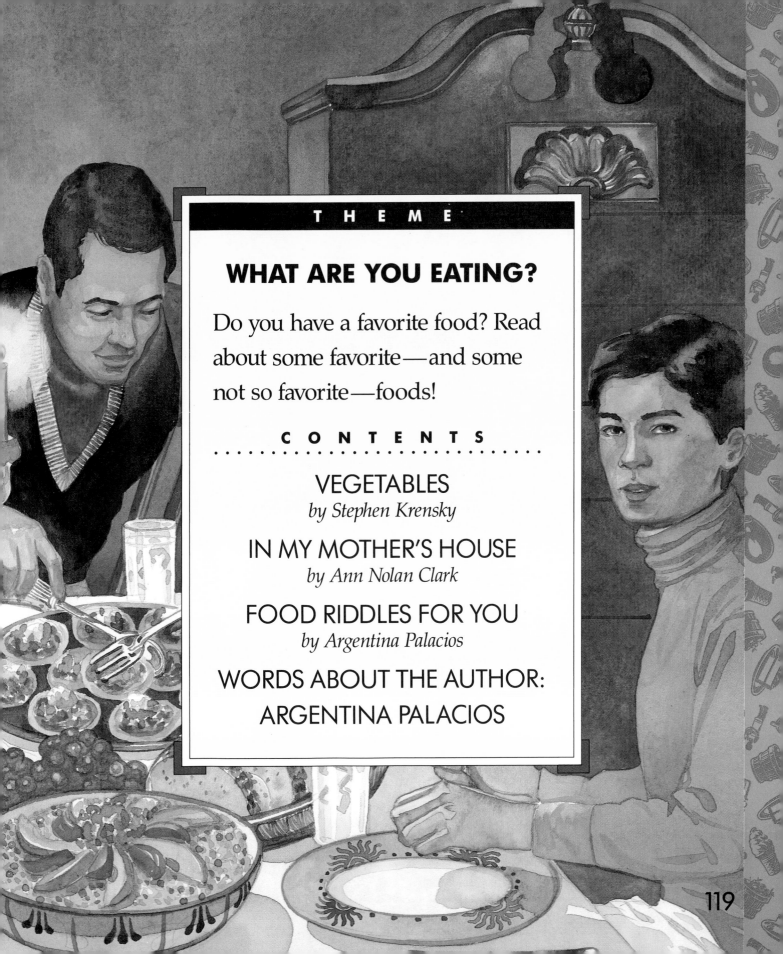

WHAT ARE YOU EATING?

Do you have a favorite food? Read about some favorite—and some not so favorite—foods!

CONTENTS

VEGETABLES

from **LIONEL AT LARGE**

by Stephen Krensky

pictures by Susanna Natti

Lionel and his family were
eating dinner.
They were having hamburgers.
Lionel liked to eat around the edge of
his roll before biting into the middle.
The middle was covered with ketchup.
"Wipe your face, Lionel," said Mother.
"It's covered with ketchup."

Lionel used his napkin.

"What about Louise?" he asked.

His big sister smiled at him.

"My face is clean," said Louise.

"I never make a mess at the table."

She carefully ate a green bean.

It was her last one.

Lionel's plate was still full
of green beans.

He stared at them.

"Eat your vegetables, Lionel," said Father.

His father always ate everything.

"There's no room for them,"
said Lionel.

"You had room for your hamburger,"
said Mother.

She always ate everything too.

"That was different," said Lionel.

"Oh?" said Mother.

Lionel looked down at his stomach.

"I have shelves in here," he explained.

"They hold the food I eat."

Lionel felt one rib.

"Here is my hamburger shelf," he said.

Lionel felt another rib.

"Here is my bread shelf," he said.

"What about your vegetable shelf?" asked Father.

Lionel felt both sides.

"I don't have one," he said.

"Hmmmph!" said Louise.

"If Lionel says he doesn't have a
vegetable shelf," said Father,
"I believe him."

"So do I," said Mother. "And we can't
expect him to eat his vegetables if he
has no place to put them."

Lionel smiled.

"Time for dessert," said Mother.

"Hooray!" said Lionel.

"Too bad you can't have any, Lionel,"
said Father.

"What do you mean?" Lionel asked.

"I've read a lot about these shelves,"
said Father. "The books say that
if you have no vegetable shelf, you have
no dessert shelf either."

"Hooray," said Louise. "Now there will
be more for me."

Lionel felt his ribs again.

"Wait!" he shouted. "I think
I found my vegetable shelf.
It was hidden under the bread shelf."

He began eating his beans.

"See," he said. "I was right."

"How lucky," said Father.

"That was a close call," said Mother.

Lionel thought so too.

THINK IT OVER

1. What did Lionel tell his parents? What did Lionel's parents tell him?

2. Do you think Lionel's food shelf idea was a good one? Why or why not?

WRITE

What food shelves do you have? Write some sentences that tell about them.

In My Mother's House

BY ANN NOLAN CLARK

Red chili and meat and melons
and yellow cornmeal
I have to eat.

Apricots and peaches
And little red plums
I have to eat.

Big round tortillas
And brown frijoles
I have to eat.
I eat them;
I like them.

ILLUSTRATED BY VELINO HERRERA

129

FOOD RIDDLES FOR YOU

from Peanut Butter, Apple Butter, Cinnamon Toast

by Argentina Palacios
pictures by Ben Mahan

Peanut butter, apple butter,
cinnamon toast.

What are the foods we like
the most?

Peanut butter, apple butter,
gingerbread man.

Guess our riddles if you can.

Red sauce on white noodles.

Grate on lots of cheese.

Don't you want that meatball?

Pass it to me, please.

What is it?

Spaghetti

It's fluffy, white, and crunchy—
A perfect movie treat.
You pop it in a popper,
Then scoop some up to eat.
What is it?

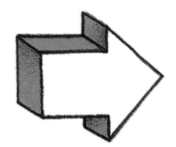

Popcorn

This fruit is long and yellow,
A monkey's favorite meal.
You can eat one anytime,
But first take off the peel.
What is it?

135

A banana

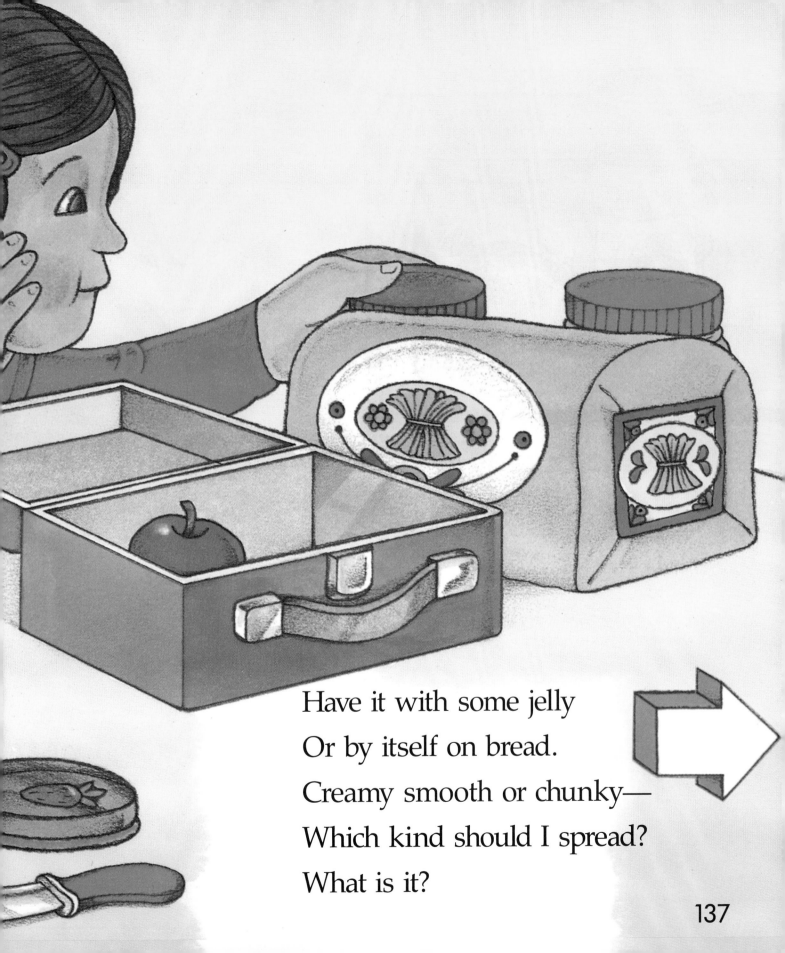

Have it with some jelly
Or by itself on bread.
Creamy smooth or chunky—
Which kind should I spread?
What is it?

137

Peanut butter

Peanut butter, apple butter, cinnamon toast.
What are the foods YOU like the most?

Words About the Author:

Argentina Palacios

Do you like guessing games? Riddles are guessing games that are fun for everyone. Argentina Palacios wrote <u>Peanut Butter, Apple Butter, Cinnamon Toast</u> because she enjoys riddles too. She was born in Panama, a country in Central America. She now lives in New York City. She writes books in English and Spanish.

You might enjoy another riddle book that Argentina Palacios helped write. Look for <u>This Can Lick a Lollipop</u> at the library.

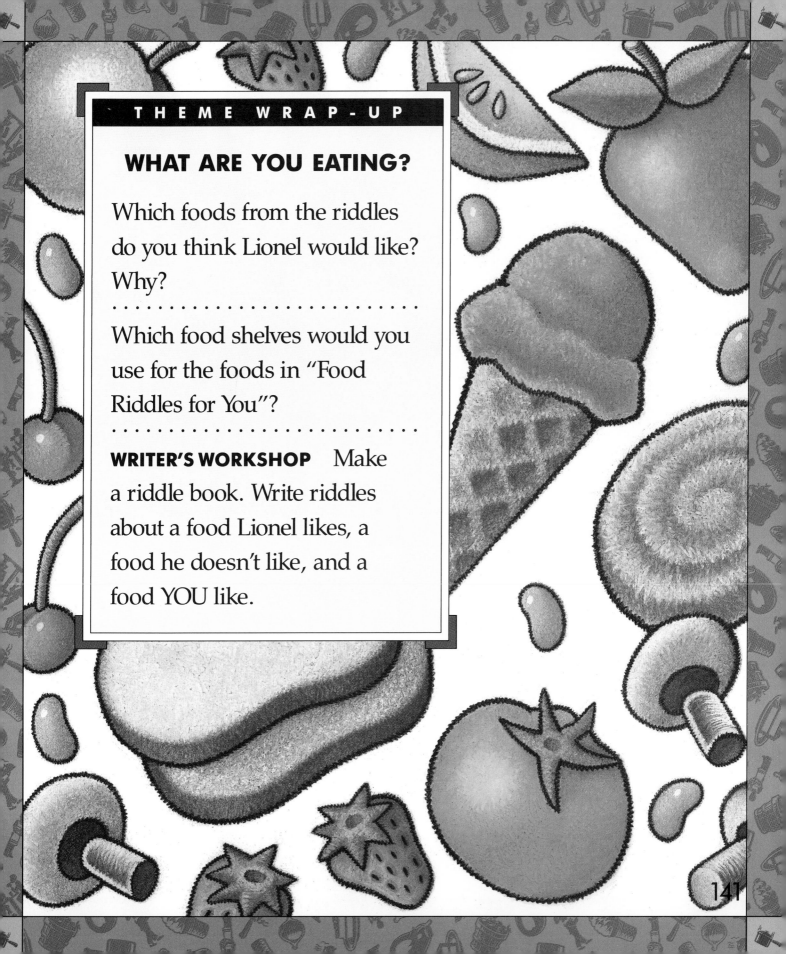

WHAT ARE YOU EATING?

Which foods from the riddles do you think Lionel would like? Why?

· ·

Which food shelves would you use for the foods in "Food Riddles for You"?

· ·

WRITER'S WORKSHOP   Make a riddle book. Write riddles about a food Lionel likes, a food he doesn't like, and a food YOU like.

141

143

Cookies

FROM FROG AND TOAD TOGETHER

by Arnold Lobel

Toad baked some cookies.
"These cookies smell very good,"
said Toad.
He ate one.
"And they taste even better," he said.
Toad ran to Frog's house.
"Frog, Frog," cried Toad,
"taste these cookies
that I have made."

Frog ate one of the cookies.
"These are the best cookies
I have ever eaten!" said Frog.

Frog and Toad ate many cookies,
one after another.
"You know, Toad," said Frog,
with his mouth full,
"I think we should stop eating.
We will soon be sick."

"You are right," said Toad.
"Let us eat one last cookie,
and then we will stop."
Frog and Toad ate
one last cookie.
There were many cookies
left in the bowl.
"Frog," said Toad,
"let us eat one very last cookie,
and then we will stop."
Frog and Toad
ate one very last cookie.

"We must stop eating!" cried Toad
as he ate another.

"Yes," said Frog, reaching for a cookie,
"we need will power."

"What is will power?" asked Toad.

"Will power is trying hard *not* to
do something that you really want
to do," said Frog.

"You mean like trying *not* to eat all
of these cookies?" asked Toad.

"Right," said Frog.

Frog put the cookies in a box.

"There," he said.

"Now we will not eat any more cookies."

"But we can open the box,"
said Toad.

"That is true," said Frog.

Frog tied some string around the box.

"There," he said.

"Now we will not eat any more
cookies."

"But we can cut the string
and open the box," said Toad.

"That is true," said Frog.

Frog got a ladder.
He put the box up on a high shelf.
"There," said Frog.
"Now we will not eat
any more cookies."

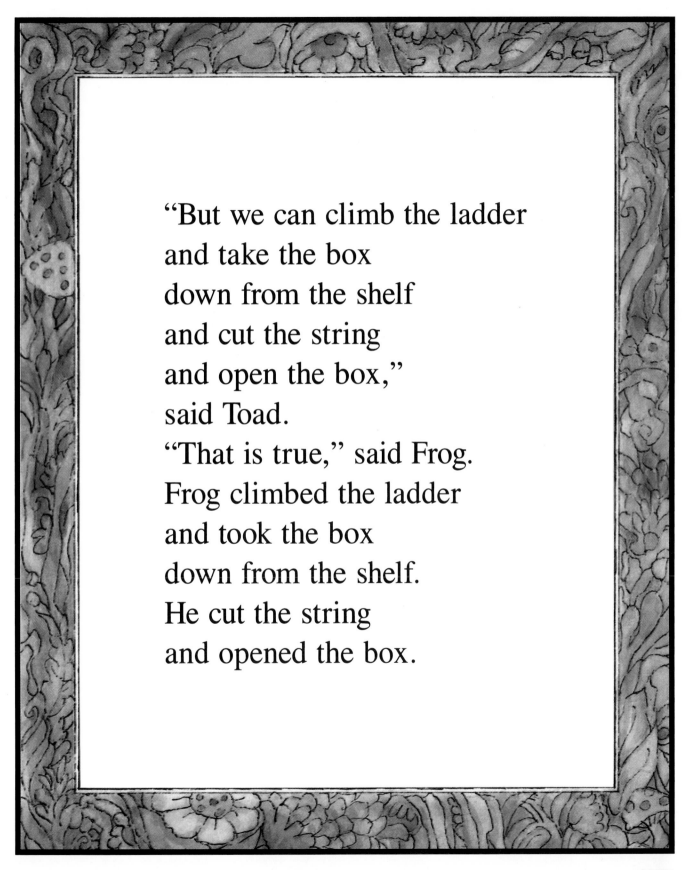

"But we can climb the ladder
and take the box
down from the shelf
and cut the string
and open the box,"
said Toad.
"That is true," said Frog.
Frog climbed the ladder
and took the box
down from the shelf.
He cut the string
and opened the box.

Frog took the box outside.
He shouted in a loud voice,
"HEY BIRDS, HERE ARE COOKIES!"
Birds came from everywhere.
They picked up all the cookies
in their beaks and flew away.
"Now we have no more cookies to eat,"
said Toad sadly.
"Not even one."
"Yes," said Frog, "but we have
lots and lots of will power."

"You may keep it all, Frog," said Toad.
"I am going home now to bake a cake."

THINK IT OVER

1. How do you know that Frog and Toad liked cookies?

2. How would you have helped Frog and Toad with their problem?

WRITE

Add to the story. Tell what you think Toad will do with the cake.

COOKIES
by Marchette Chute

If I had a kitchen
　　And knew how to bake,
These are the cookies
　　I would make:
Chocolate, peanut,
　　Lemon and spice—
All the ones
　　That are extra nice.
And to everyone on the block I'd say,
"Here are the cookies I made today.
Come and eat them right away."

illustrated by Kid Kane

COOKIE CUTTERS
by Mary Ann Hoberman

AWARD-WINNING
POET

Cookie cutters
Cutting cookies
Cutting different
Shapes and sizes
First you make them
Next you bake them
Then you take them
And you cool them
And . . .
That's weird.
They've disappeared!

The Doorbell Rang
by Pat Hutchins

"I've made some cookies for tea," said Ma.

"Good," said Victoria and Sam. "We're starving."

"Share them between yourselves," said Ma.

"I made plenty."

"That's six each," said Sam and Victoria.

"They look as good as Grandma's," said Victoria.

"They smell as good as Grandma's," said Sam.

"No one makes cookies like Grandma,"
said Ma as the doorbell rang.

It was Tom and Hannah from next door.

"Come in," said Ma.

"You can share the cookies."

"That's three each," said Sam and Victoria.

"They smell as good as your Grandma's," said Tom.

"And they look as good," said Hannah.

"No one makes cookies like Grandma,"
said Ma as the doorbell rang.
It was Peter and his little brother.
"Come in," said Ma.
"You can share the cookies."

"That's two each," said Victoria and Sam.
"They look as good as your Grandma's,"
said Peter. "And smell as good."

"Nobody makes cookies like Grandma,"
said Ma as the doorbell rang.
It was Joy and Simon
with their four cousins.
"Come in," said Ma.
"You can share the cookies."

"That's one each," said Sam and Victoria.

"They smell as good as your Grandma's," said Joy.

"And look as good," said Simon.

"No one makes cookies like Grandma,"
said Ma as the doorbell rang and rang.
"Oh dear," said Ma as the children stared
at the cookies on their plates.
"Perhaps you'd better eat them
before we open the door."
"We'll wait," said Sam.

It was Grandma with an
enormous tray of cookies.

"How nice to have so many friends to share them with," said Grandma. "It's a good thing I made a lot!"

"And no one makes cookies like Grandma,"
said Ma as the doorbell rang.

THINK IT OVER

1. How many cookies did Ma make? How do you know?

2. Who do you think rang the doorbell at the end of the story?

WRITE

Write about the cookies Ma made. Tell how they looked, smelled, and tasted.

MORE COOKIES, PLEASE

How could the children from " The Doorbell Rang " have helped Frog and Toad?

. . . .

What do you think Toad and Frog would do if Ma and the children rang their doorbell?

. . . .

WRITER'S WORKSHOP If you could visit Frog and Toad or Ma and the children, what would you take to them? Write a story about your visit. Draw a picture, too.

169

CONNECTIONS

GEORGE WASHINGTON CARVER

Do you like soup? Bread? Ice cream? Did you know that these foods can be made from peanuts? It's true! George Washington Carver learned that peanuts can be used to make many things.

Dr. Carver was a great teacher and scientist. He spent his whole life helping others.

■ Write a sentence telling how you help others. Draw a picture to go with it.

COMMUNITY HELPERS

Name some people who help others. What do they do to help? Write what you know on word webs like these.

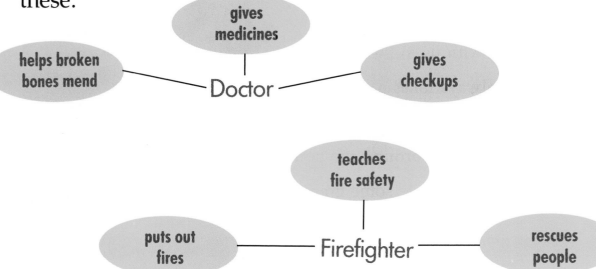

gives medicines

helps broken bones mend

Doctor

gives checkups

teaches fire safety

puts out fires

Firefighter

rescues people

MATH CONNECTION

PEANUT PROBLEMS

Peanuts grow in shells. Most shells hold two peanuts. Imagine that you open three peanut shells. How many peanuts will you find? Write your own peanut problem. Have a classmate find the answer.

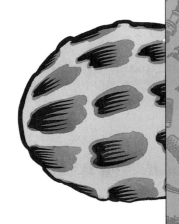

GLOSSARY

A

about   Let's talk **about** our trip to the park.

after   I brush my teeth **after** I eat.

along   Come **along** with us to the beach.

always   The baby **always** takes a nap.

any   I don't have **any** wings, but a bird does.

around   The grass grew all **around** the pond.

ate   Lee was hungry, so he **ate** some grapes.

after

around

B

beach   At the **beach** we play in the sand and swim.

been   We have **been** to the zoo five times.

before   The sun comes up **before** I wake up.

better   I like to play **better** than I like to sleep.

biting   The cat is **biting** into the cheese.

boat   It is fun to ride in a **boat** on the lake.

bright   It is very **bright** with all the lights on.

bushes   The **bushes** grow by our home.

beach

C

cake   We will eat all the **cake.**

children   Dad read a story to the **children.**

climb   Let's **climb** up the steps.

count   The little girl can **count** to ten.

cry   The baby began to **cry.**

children

D

dear   Kim said, "Oh, **dear!**" when she saw the mess.

doesn't   A cat **doesn't** have wings, but a bird does.

door   Chen came to our **door** and rang the bell.

door

E

each   Rosa and Mike waved to **each** other.

egg   Dad cooked an **egg** for me.

ever   That is the best bike I have **ever** seen.

everyone   We all liked the show, so **everyone** clapped.

egg

F

flew   The bird **flew** to the tree.

flipped   She **flipped** her feet up and down in the water.

food   Eating **food** helps you grow.

front   The dog dug a hole with its **front** paws.

front

G

goes   My mom **goes** to work each day.

grew   The little puppy **grew** into a big dog.

H

has   Pat **has** a horse.

having   We are **having** milk with dinner.

held   Dad picked up the baby and **held** her close.

hold   Let's **hold** hands as we cross the street.

home   A **home** is a nice place to live.

held

home

174

I

I've   **I've** been playing with my friends.

J

just   We **just** missed the bus.

K

keep   **Keep** on walking fast.

knows   Jerome **knows** how to swim.

L

laid   The hen **laid** eggs in her nest.

last   The boy at the end of the line was **last.**

laughed   I **laughed** at the funny pigs.

liked   Matt **liked** to wear his red hat.

laughed

laid

M

made   Gina **made** a hat out of paper.

many   **Many** boys and girls go to our school.

may   **May** I go out to play?

made

N

next   Tom was **next** in line.

nice   We had a **nice** time at the zoo.

night   Anna goes to sleep at **night.**

nobody   The school was closed, so **nobody** was there.

night

O

oh   **Oh,** this kitten is so soft!

only   There was **only** one peach left.

only

P

perhaps   **Perhaps** we can play outside today.

planted   We **planted** the seeds by the tree.

R

rang   When the bell **rang,** it was time to eat.

real   I saw a **real** bear at the zoo.

river   Fish live in the **river.**

S

safe   You are **safe** when you use a seat belt.

sail   We will **sail** the boat on the lake.

shelf   Nathan put the book on the **shelf.**

should   We **should** pick up this mess.

shouted   Jack **shouted** my name from across the park.

show   **Show** us your new dog.

shelf

side   Carmen rode her sled down the **side** of the hill.

some   There are **some** ducks on the lake.

someday   **Someday** you will have a job.

something   Smiling is **something** you do when you are happy.

spot   We picked a **spot** on the grass and sat down.

stand   Peter sat down, but Ann told him to **stand** up.

stop   **Stop** and look both ways before you cross the street.

stop

T

their   The girls clap **their** hands.

them   Meg sat with her pets and played with **them.**

these   **These** books are mine, and those are yours.

think   I **think** I know where my hat is.

three   My **three** friends are Jan, Taro, and Tonya.

two   You have **two** hands and **two** feet.

three

W

water

wait   I had to **wait** for the school bus.

want   I **want** to see my friends today.

water   The **water** in the tub was hot.

way   The **way** to school is down this street.

wear   I **wear** socks on my feet.

we're   They want Jan and me to play, so **we're** going now.

whale   A **whale** is the biggest animal in the sea.

woman   Mrs. Jones is a nice **woman.**

wrong   I got lost when I went the **wrong** way.

wear

whale

Y

---

you're   We are glad **you're** here to play.

yourselves   You boys will have to play by **yourselves.**